T5-AOA-332

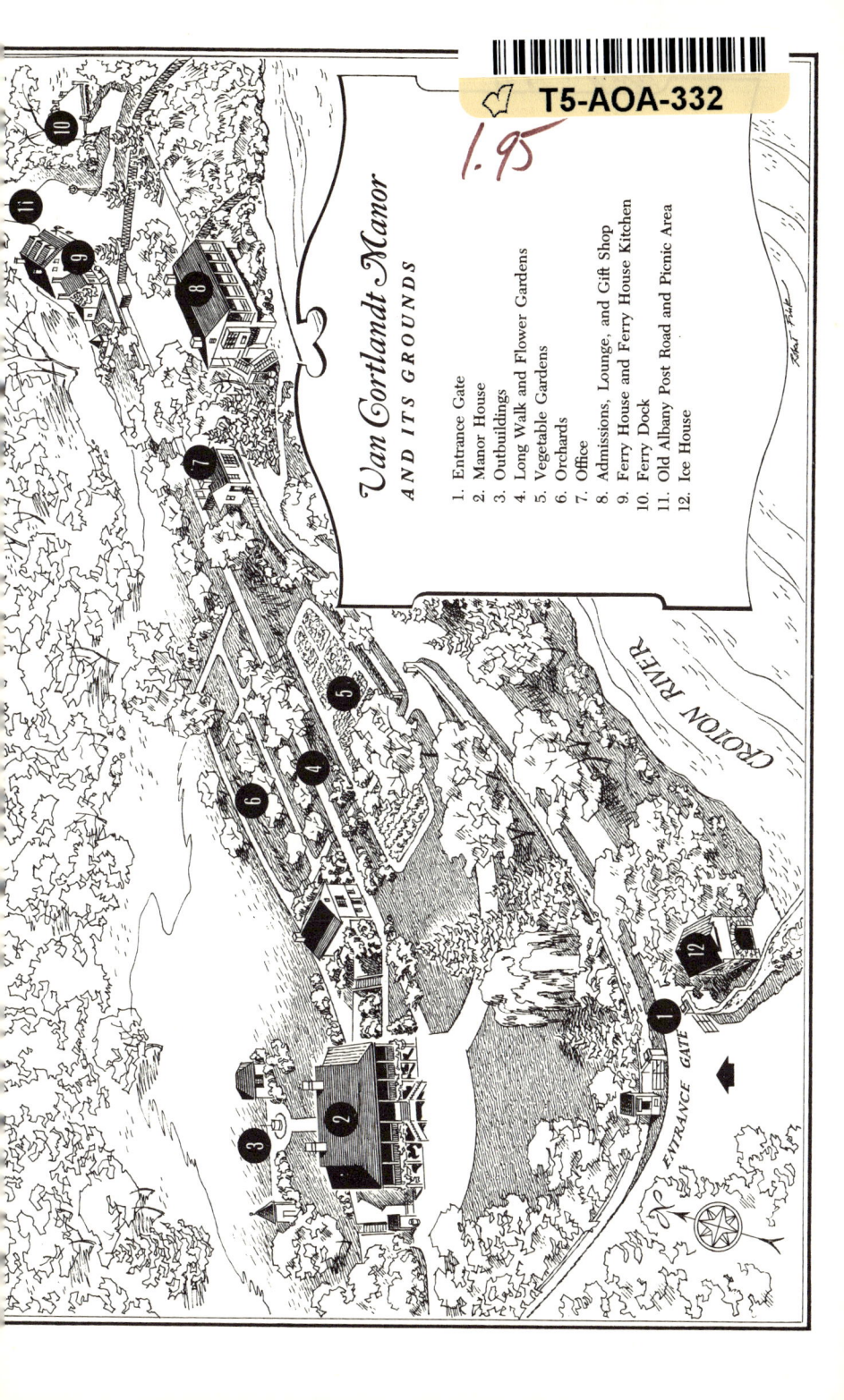

1.95

Van Cortlandt Manor
AND ITS GROUNDS

1. Entrance Gate
2. Manor House
3. Outbuildings
4. Long Walk and Flower Gardens
5. Vegetable Gardens
6. Orchards
7. Office
8. Admissions, Lounge, and Gift Shop
9. Ferry House and Ferry House Kitchen
10. Ferry Dock
11. Old Albany Post Road and Picnic Area
12. Ice House

CROTON RIVER

ENTRANCE GATE

North or rear elevation of manor house, showing well.

A SLEEPY HOLLOW RESTORATIONS GUIDEBOOK

VAN CORTLANDT MANOR

by Joseph T. Butler

SLEEPY HOLLOW RESTORATIONS
Tarrytown · *New York*

Illustrations except as otherwise noted are from the collections of Sleepy Hollow Restorations.

Sleepy Hollow Restorations, Incorporated, is a nonprofit educational institution chartered by the State of New York. It was established under an endowment provided by the late John D. Rockefeller, Jr. Sleepy Hollow Restorations owns and maintains Van Cortlandt Manor, in Croton-on-Hudson, a distinguished eighteenth-century family residence; Sunnyside, Washington Irving's picturesque home in Tarrytown; and Philipsburg Manor, Upper Mills, an impressive example of a colonial commercial-mill complex in North Tarrytown.

Library of Congress Cataloging in Publication Data

Butler, Joseph T.   Van Cortlandt Manor

(A Sleepy Hollow Restorations guidebook)
Bibliography: p.
1. Van Cortlandt Manor.   2. Van Cortlandt family.
I. Title.   II. Series: Sleepy Hollow Restorations,
Tarrytown, N.Y. A Sleepy Hollow Restorations guidebook.
F127.W5B87   974.7'277 [B]   77-17531
ISBN 0-912882-33-6

Copyright © 1978 by Sleepy Hollow Restorations, Inc.

All rights reserved.
For information, address the publisher:
Sleepy Hollow Restorations, Inc.
Tarrytown, New York 10591

ISBN 0-912882-33-6, paper
Library of Congress Catalog Card Number: 77-17531

Printed in the United States of America
Designed by Ray Freiman

ARMS OF VAN CORTLANDT.

1. Coat of arms of the Van Cortlandt family. Painted in oil on a wood panel, signed by G. Kane, probably a painter of coach doors, about whom little is known. This dates from the late eighteenth or early nineteenth century. The coat of arms was adopted by Oloff Van Cortlandt before his death in 1684; it was accompanied by the motto, *Virtus sibi munus* (Virtue through Service).

The Van Cortlandt Family Bible (see page 6), on display in the Old Parlor, was printed in Dordrecht and Amsterdam in 1710. It was inscribed in 1744 by Philip Van Cortlandt, son of Stephanus Van Cortlandt, and contains a notice of his death in 1748.

Genealogy of the Van Cortlandt Family

Oloff Van Cortlandt, who came to America from Holland in 1638, married Annetje Loockermans. Their oldest son was Stephanus.

Stephanus Van Cortlandt   1643–1700
   (Mayor of New York)   m. 1671   Gertruyd Schuyler   1654–1723
   (14 children)

Philip Van Cortlandt   1683–1748
   (6 children)   m. 1710   Catherine DePeyster   1688–1734

Pierre Van Cortlandt   1721–1814   m. 1748   Joanna Livingston   1722–1808
(Lieutenant Governor of New York)
   (8 children)

   (Brigadier-General of The Continental Army)
   Philip Van Cortlandt   1749–1831

Pierre Van Cortlandt, Jr.   1762–1848
   (1 child)   m. 1801   1. Catherine Clinton Taylor   1770–1811
         m. 1813   2. Anne Stevenson   1774–1821

Pierre Van Cortlandt III   1815–1884
   (7 children)   m. 1836   Catherine Elizabeth Beck   1818–1895

         Anne Van Cortlandt   1847–1940

Catherine Van Cortlandt   1838–1921
         m. 1873   John R. Mathews   1835–1898

Costumed guides await visitors outside the lower entrance at Van Cortlandt Manor

The History

VAN CORTLANDT MANOR is that very rare American phenomenon: a residence occupied by the same family for virtually two and a half centuries. On the present manor house site, the first building was erected by the Van Cortlandts early in the eighteenth century, and their uninterrupted occupancy lasted until almost the middle of the twentieth. This is fully documented through the survival, and later restoration, of its landscape, architecture, and interior furnishings.

Located at the confluence of the Croton and Hudson rivers, the property is some forty miles north of New York City, and the manor faces south down the broad Hudson toward today's metropolis. This has always been a strategic position for both river and land travel: indeed, the old Albany Post Road worked its way across the manor.

Before the advent of European settlers, the beautiful and picturesque countryside was occupied by the Kitchawanc Indians, part of one of the Algonquin nations. It is believed that one of the earliest buildings on the manor was originally set up as a trading post with the Indians.

The acquisition of the property and development of the manor by the Van Cortlandts were part and parcel of the guiding drive of the early settlers, determined to expand their area of trade according to the inspired mercantilism of their time.

The Dutch West India Company had been involved in the creation of what was known as Nieuw Netherland. In order to encourage agriculture and the settlement of the upcountry by private enterprise rather than expenditure of company funds, it issued in 1629 a document known as *The Charter of Privileges and Exemptions.*

Under the provisions of this charter, the company agreed, among other things, to grant vast tracts of land, known as patroonships, to any of its stockholders who would establish a settlement of fifty adults upon them within a period of four years from their expression of intent. The amounts of land and the powers conferred to these new patroons were, in reality, nothing but an extension of old feudal privileges.

When, in 1664, the English took over what they referred to as New York, they maintained these provisions, albeit with certain modifications based on the English manor system. Between 1671 and 1701, six such manors were chartered in Westchester County. As the program was administered, it was the outstanding merchants who, having adequate means, were given the opportunity to acquire these large estates. The result was a further concentration of the existing wealth in the hands of a few and the creation of a powerful landed aristocracy.

Thus it was that the great accumulation of Van Cortlandt

holdings originated. Oloff, the first of the name to come to the New World, had arrived in Nieuw Amsterdam in 1638 as a soldier with the West India Company. In 1642, he married Annetje Loockermans, and purchased a "burgher right."

In order to increase commercial activity in the settlement, the Company had had a policy of permitting individual traders to operate out of the port of Nieuw Amsterdam. To qualify for such a privilege, an individual had to acquire a business license, known as a burgher right, which authorized him not only to engage in trade but also to enjoy all the rights of a "free citizen" of the town.

As Oloff prospered, he held a number of public and political posts, and was in fact one of the three commissioners chosen to negotiate the terms of surrender to the British. When he died, in 1684, he had come to be considered the fourth wealthiest individual in New York. As a free burgher, he had adopted a coat of arms with the four sails of a windmill saltirewise (that is, crossed in an X) among five mullets, with the motto *Virtus sibi munus* (Virtue through service) (Illus. 1).

Oloff fathered seven children, whose marriages were to align them with some of the most important of the other leading New York families. The eldest son, Stephanus (1643–1700), prominent as merchant, soldier, jurist, and legislator, was a member of the Governor's Council and appointed Mayor of New York by Sir Edmund Andros in 1677, when only thirty-four years old. He was the first native-born mayor of the city.

Stephanus's desire to increase his land holdings led him into Dutchess and Richmond counties in New York; as well as into New Jersey and Pennsylvania. In 1683, he turned his attention to Westchester County, and in 1688 and 1695 bought parcels of land that extended from Croton Point beyond Peekskill.

Van Cortlandt Manor was chartered by Royal Patent during the reign of William III, on June 17, 1697, encompassing at the time some 86,123 acres. It was bounded on the south by Philipsburg Manor, on the north by what is now the Westchester-Putnam county line, on the east by the long-disputed New York-Connecticut boundary line, and on the west by the Hudson River (Illus. 2). Stephanus Van Cortlandt also owned fifteen hundred acres across the Hudson, on its west side.

According to family tradition, it was apparently during Stephanus's ownership that a building was constructed on the property at Croton. But, with his death, the manor passed into the control of Stephanus's wife, the former Gertruyd Schuyler. She survived until 1723, and the property was to remain intact another nine years. Since the Van Cortlandts adhered to the Dutch system of inheritance, the real property was to be divided among all the heirs, regardless of sex, rather than passing in its entirety to the eldest son, as under the British system of primogeniture. However, they also observed the English form of entail, in which the land in each division descended through the male line.

2. The charter granted by King William III of England to Stephanus Van Cortlandt, creating the Manor of Cortlandt in 1697. It outlines the boundaries of the grant as well as the privileges and perquisites appertaining thereto. →

Gulielmus Tertius Dei gratia
Know
Yee
To have
And
Mannor
And
And
And
To have
Witness
In Testimony

In 1732, Philip Verplanck, a grandson of Stephanus, made a survey of the land, and it was subsequently divided among ten living heirs. The original map showing the division of the land into numbered plots has not survived, but there is extant a copy drawn by Evert Bancker around 1775 (Illus. 3). Philip Van Cortlandt (1683–1748), third son of Stephanus and his oldest surviving male heir, inherited the property on which the manor house stands. In all, his domain consisted of about ten thousand acres.

3. In 1775, Evert Bancker drew this copy of a map originally made in 1732 by Philip Verplanck, showing division of the manor into lots among the ten living heirs. (The original map does not survive, but this pre-Revolutionary copy is in the Sleepy Hollow Restorations collection.) →

THE MANNOR of CORTLAND

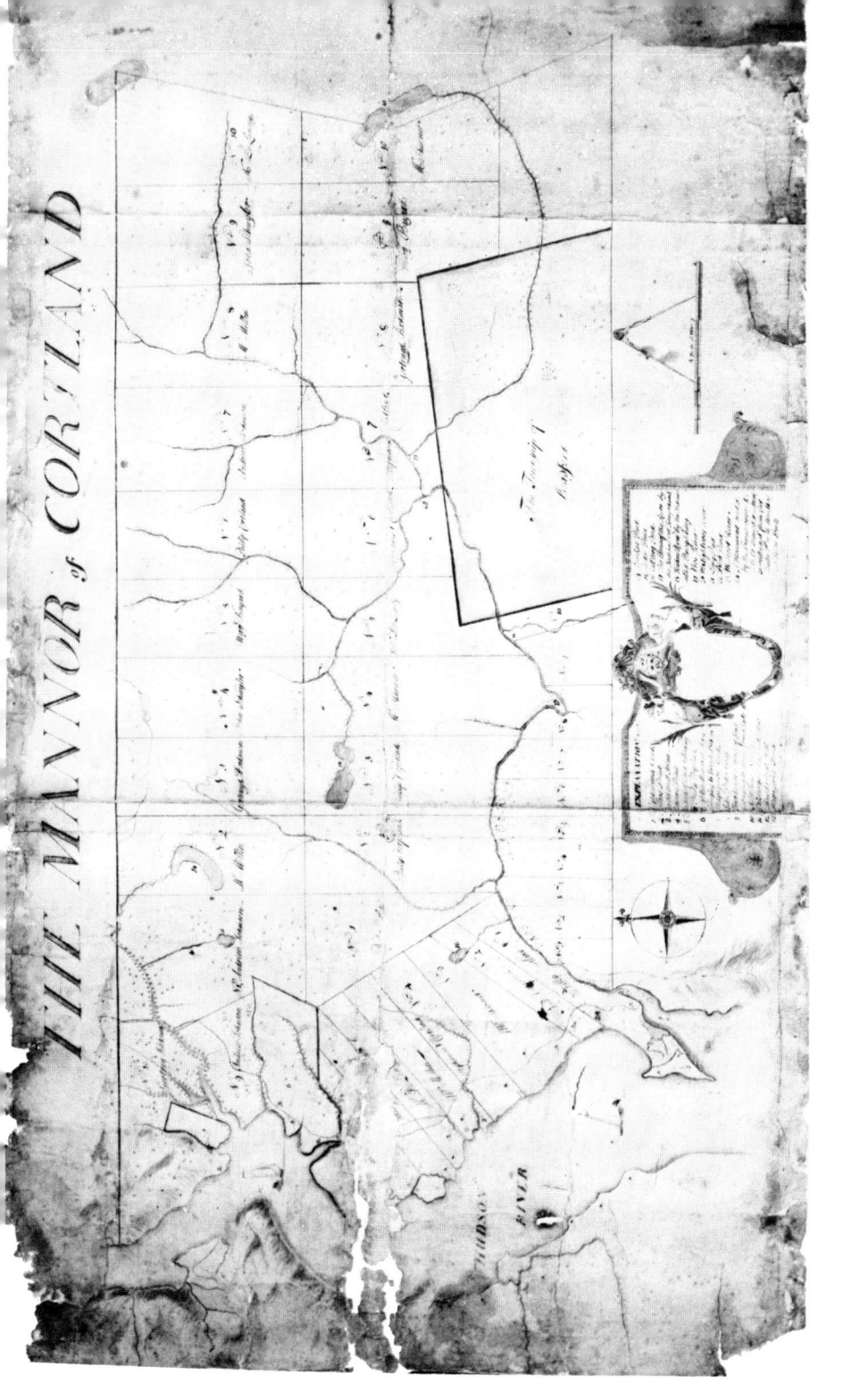

Like others of his family, Philip, a merchant, held many public offices. In 1710, he had married Catharine De Peyster, whose father was also a wealthy merchant and a former Mayor of New York. She bore six children, five of them boys. While continuing to maintain their principal residence in New York City, they and their children spent an increasing amount of time at the manor and effected improvements in it. The sons, Stephen, Abraham, Philip, John, and Pierre, were much concerned with all activities in and around the manor (Illus. 4, 5).

Catharine Van Cortlandt died in 1734, and upon her husband's death fourteen years later only two of their children, Stephen and Pierre, survived. The New York City properties went to Stephen, along with several farms and a lot on the manor. But it was Pierre (1721–1814) who inherited the manor house lot, comprising 1225 acres and "the ferry House and Ferry thereunto belonging including the farme where David Brown now lives on also a lott of land . . . in the possession of Peter Williams and the Widow of Hendrick Davids."[1] We thus know with certainty that the ferry house had already been built and was in operation at this time.

4 & 5. Abraham Van Cortlandt (1713–1746), top, painted about 1720, and Pierre Van Cortlandt (1721–1814), bottom, painted about 1730. These two and John (1718–1747), three of the children of Philip and Catharine DePeyster Van Cortlandt, were done in oil on canvas by itinerant portraitists of the Hudson River Valley, using English mezzotint sources for backgrounds. The portraits are in their original wood-and-gesso gilt frames, Abraham's in the manor house, Pierre's and John's in the collection of the Brooklyn Museum.

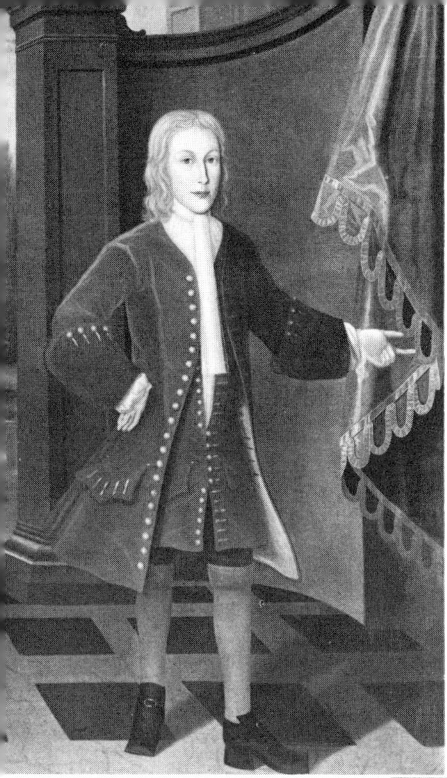

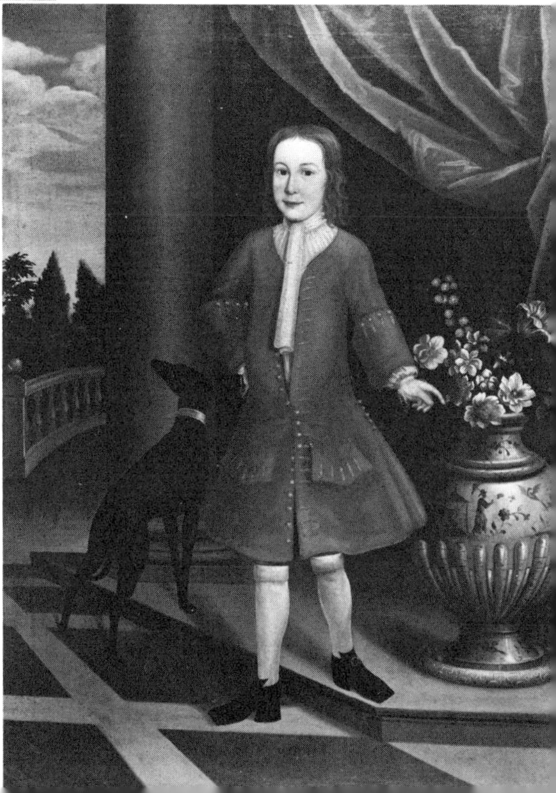

In 1748, Pierre married his cousin, Joanna Livingston (Illus. 6). In 1750, with their infant son Philip, they moved from New York City to the house in Croton, which was now to be their permanent home. Pierre had grown up surrounded by wealth, in a family prominent in both politics and trade. Shortly after his son's birth, he was elected a tax assessor in New York City's South Ward, but held the position for less than a year. This was his only elected office prior to his campaigning for a seat in the Provincial General Assembly eighteen years later.

When Pierre and his family moved to the manor house in 1749, it probably consisted of a central core some thirty by forty feet in size, built into the hillside as was customary with seventeenth-century Dutch settlers. We know that Pierre employed plasterers and masons in 1749, and again in 1760, and architectural historians relate that the house was then expanded with four rooms on the main floor, three on the ground floor, and a top floor with several large spaces. Two huge brick chimneys provided ample draught for the fireplaces constructed beneath them. A porch on three sides of the main floor gave a gracious flavor to the house—but neither then nor since did the building ever lose the basic quality of a farmhouse.

Numerous contemporary documents tell us of life as it went on there from the mid-eighteenth century until the Revolution. The manor, relatively self-sufficient, hospitable, and informal, was well placed for trips to both New York City and Albany. From a receipt book that Pierre began to keep in 1738, we see that in 1749 he was planting an apple orchard. Accounts starting the next year reveal that the mills were busy supplying lumber and flour for the family and for local tenants, as well as for shipment to New York City.

In 1759, Pierre bought a schooner for trade downriver to New York and upriver to Albany, and in the following year he had a scow built for the transport of grain. Family papers

6. Oil-on-canvas portrait of Joanna Livingston Van Cortlandt (1722–1808), probably painted shortly before her death by the Albany painter Ezra Ames (1768–1836). The daughter of Gilbert and Cornelia Beekman Livingston, she married Pierre Van Cortlandt in 1748.

of the period make frequent references to a periagua (in more modern spelling, a piragua), a flat-bottomed, two-masted work boat of shallow draft. The manor work force consisted largely of slaves purchased from time to time from the 1750s into the early 1800s. The women slaves did household duties, while the men worked the garden and mill and tended the farm animals. In addition, tenants and hired hands saw to the dairy and the field crops.

Beyond managing his own manor holdings, Pierre also handled the affairs of some of the other heirs, who owned parts of the property. It fell to him, too, to settle the estates of several deceased members of his family, and in order to discharge all of these responsibilities, Pierre, according to family tradition, had a separate small office structure erected near the northeast corner of the manor house.

The tranquillity of life was disturbed in the 1760s by the fact that tenants on the New York manors grew restive because there was no way they could acquire title to the properties they worked, whereas in the adjacent provinces of New Hampshire and Connecticut legal steps were available for them to become owners of their own lands. However, the upsurge of tenant resentment at Van Cortlandt Manor never reached the stage of open hostility that was to become manifest at Livingston Manor.

Pierre had still other obligations to discharge: At the outbreak of the Revolution, he was a colonel in the county militia, and thus required to recruit for his regiment. He had also been responsible for providing a church and school for his own family and those of the manorial tenants. In 1767, St. Peter's, a one-room wooden church, was built on land at Peekskill; this was apparently the church closest to the manor at that time. According to Philip Van Cortlandt's *Memoir*, a small one-room schoolhouse was also built around 1760, "about half a mile from the house." Here, the eight children born to Pierre and Joanna, as well as "a

7. General Philip Van Cortlandt (1749–1831), painted in oil on canvas by Ezra Ames, around his sixtieth birthday in 1809. It is now the property of the Metropolitan Museum of Art, gift of Christian A. Zabriskie, 1940.

few children of the neighbours [were taught] by a Common Schoolmaster, to read, write badly and something of arithmatick . . . "[2]

Philip (1749–1831) was the eldest son, and after brief academic training he returned to assist his father in managing the estate business (Illus. 7). With the manor becoming a thriving community, much of his time seems to have gone into surveying activities, mill operations, and the running of a retail store. A 1779 tax list recorded the names of 550 taxable Van Cortlandt Manor inhabitants. But many changes, of course, were to be wrought by the war.

A sharp division of political attitudes existed at the time; many of Pierre's in-laws were Loyalists, as indeed were his neighbors to the south, the Philipses. In 1774, Governor William Tryon of New York visited Croton to try to persuade Pierre to remain loyal to the English King, even holding out the promise of more land and a title of nobility. His son, Philip, was offered a major's commission in the British army. But both declined.

Thenceforth, the Van Cortlandts played an important role in the patriotic cause and became deeply involved in the war. Pierre's direct associates now became George Washington, Benjamin Franklin, and Governor George Clinton. Pierre was commissioned Colonel of the Third Westchester County Regiment in 1775; Philip became a Lieutenant Colonel in the Fourth New York Regiment.

In 1776, as part of a reorganization of the army, General Washington made Philip Colonel of the Second New York Regiment. And as the war progressed, Philip was to serve under the command of Lafayette in several campaigns and become his good friend. He fought at Saratoga and was an eyewitness to the surrender of Burgoyne. He also fought on the New York frontier, where England's Indian allies, under the leadership of the Mohawk chief Joseph Brant (Illus. 8), were causing considerable trouble. At the final Battle of Yorktown, in 1871, Philip was in command of the Second New York Regiment, and in September 1783 he was elevated to the rank of Brigadier General (Illus. 9).

The events of the war were directly reflected at the manor. In 1776, the mill was requisitioned to make flour around the clock for the Continental Army, a requirement so urgent that some millers were exempted from military

8. Colonel Joseph Brant (Thayendanegea), Indian leader who played an important role in the Mohawk Valley campaigns, painted by Ezra Ames in 1806, a year before Brant's death. The portrait, which originally hung in the manor house at Croton, is now owned by the New York State Historical Society, Cooperstown, N.Y.

9. Philip Van Cortlandt in his Revolutionary War uniform, in a pastel portrait by James Sharples (1751?–1811). It is now in the Independence National Park Collection, Philadelphia.

service. After the evacuation of New York and the Battle of White Plains (October 1776), a portion of Washington's forces withdrew north of the Croton River, into the hills. This small force was positioned to protect the eastern bank of the Hudson at King's Ferry, where crossing was easier and communication lines with New England could be kept open.

Pierre sat in the Second, Third, and Fourth Provincial Congresses. At the Fourth, held in White Plains, July 9, 1776, New York ratified the Declaration of Independence (Illus. 10). Pierre headed the Committee of Safety that governed the state until an election could be held in 1777, and it was he who presided over the State Provincial Convention in Kingston which drafted the first Constitution of the State of New York.

Elected Lieutenant Governor by the first Senate under the new Constitution, Pierre became acting governor for most of the war period, with Governor Clinton away as commanding general on the New York frontier. By winter 1776, the main theater of war had moved down to New Jersey and Pennsylvania, leaving Westchester free from major encounters. But now there was something perhaps even worse to be feared.

The British were quartered in New York City, and the manor was situated in what was known as the "Neutral Ground." Into that area, patrols, foragers, and raiding parties from both sides made frequent forays, looting and commandeering throughout the countryside. As early as July 1776, the Van Cortlandts sensed the danger of their position and moved north from the manor house to one in Peekskill belonging to Pierre's aged aunt, Mrs. Henry Beekman.

In 1777, in order to be closer to the State Legislature, the family moved again, this time to Rhinebeck, almost fifty miles farther north. This entailed moving not only household furnishings, but also livestock, and all kinds of supplies and provisions. It took ten weeks to complete the

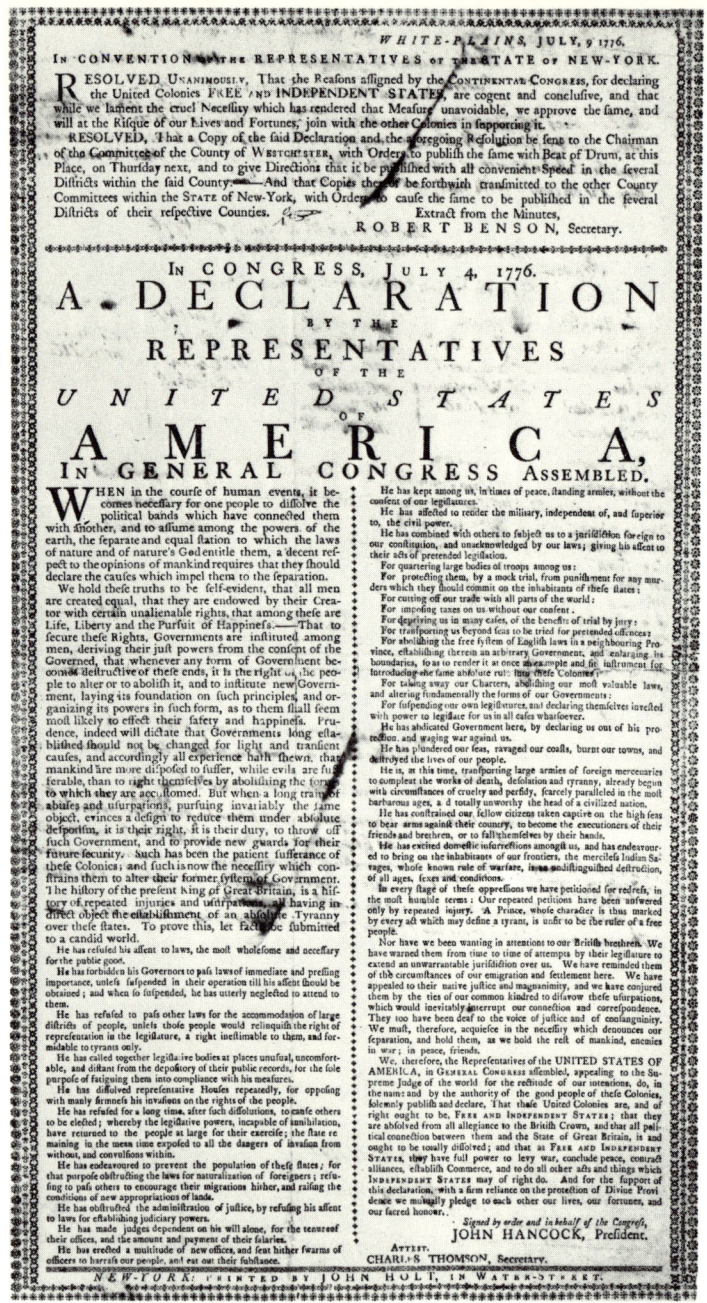

10. Printed version of the Declaration of Independence, as read at White Plains, July 9, 1776, when the Provincial Congress of which Pierre Van Cortlandt was a member ratified it for the state of New York. The original is now in the Henry E. Huntington Library and Art Gallery, San Marino, California.

operation; on July 1, the family, then including Pierre and Joanna, Pierre, Jr., Gilbert, Ann, and Catharine, arrived in Rhinebeck.

The move proved wise, for considerable plundering apparently took place at the Croton manor house. In 1779, as the British advanced up the Hudson, Pierre was to write to his son that he had learned that "The Enemy In Coming up Landed at Tellors Point When [went] to the old house at the farm & plundered Every thing they Could . . ."[3]

A memorandum drawn up by Pierre at the end of the war does indeed show that the house had been stripped of doors and shutters and the remaining furniture, and lumber had been taken from other buildings. Pierre and Joanna were not to return to Croton until after Pierre had spent some seventeen years in government service, most of it in upstate New York. Instead, they returned to Peekskill, which had been their first place of refuge in the war.

Philip, however, came back in 1783, after the peace treaty had been signed, and set about repairing the manor house. Soon after the end of hostilities, Philip served as Commissioner of Forfeiture for the Southern District of New York. Under various acts of the State Legislature in the late 1770s, real and personal property belonging to New Yorkers who remained loyal to the Crown were seized; it was the business of these commissioners to see to the eventual sale of such confiscated Loyalist holdings.

Philip faithfully discharged this task, keeping careful accounts and transmitting to governmental authorities the largest amount of sales revenue realized anywhere in the state. The only criticism of his role came during the hotly contested election of 1808, when he was anonymously accused of having speculated in State certificates. But no action was ever taken against him, so it can be assumed that this was merely an election-campaign ploy to try to defeat the Jeffersonian Republicans. Philip, meantime, had also

11. Pierre Van Cortlandt toward the end of his life, when he had again returned to the Croton manor house, painted about 1810 by John Wesley Jarvis (1780–1840).

become one of the founders of the Society of the Cincinnati.

When the British finally evacuated New York in November 1783, General Washington planned to make a glorious reentry into the city. Pierre, now Lieutenant Governor of the state, journeyed down from Peekskill for the occasion, as befitted his office. He spent the night en route with Philip at the manor house, and on November 25, 1783, Pierre wrote, "I . . . rode triumphant into the City with the Commander in Chief."[4]

Pierre remained in the same office until his retirement in 1795 (Illus. 12), only once in his eighteen-year tenure expressing any ambition to become Governor. That was in January 1789, when he publicly announced that a number of friends had urged him to run for Governor in the upcoming election. In doing so, Pierre added his name to the list of those who wished to unseat George Clinton. The latter had led the New York forces opposed to the Federal Constitution of 1787 and continued the fight until July 28, 1788, when New York State voted ratification.

This opposition had gained Clinton the undying antagonism of Alexander Hamilton, and Pierre judged that with this development the time might be ripe for him to make a bid for the governorship. However, when Hamilton threw his support to Robert Yates, Pierre was persuaded to withdraw. He never again attempted to unseat Governor Clinton. After retiring from office, Pierre once again devoted more time to management of the family estates and business involvements.

It was at about this time that he built the Methodist Bethel Chapel, a one-story clapboard building north of the manor house, on the old Albany Post Road (Illus. 13), donating the land for both the chapel and the adjoining cemetery. The chapel, still in use, has been designated a National Historic Landmark. And it was Pierre who authorized the holding of camp meetings on his property.

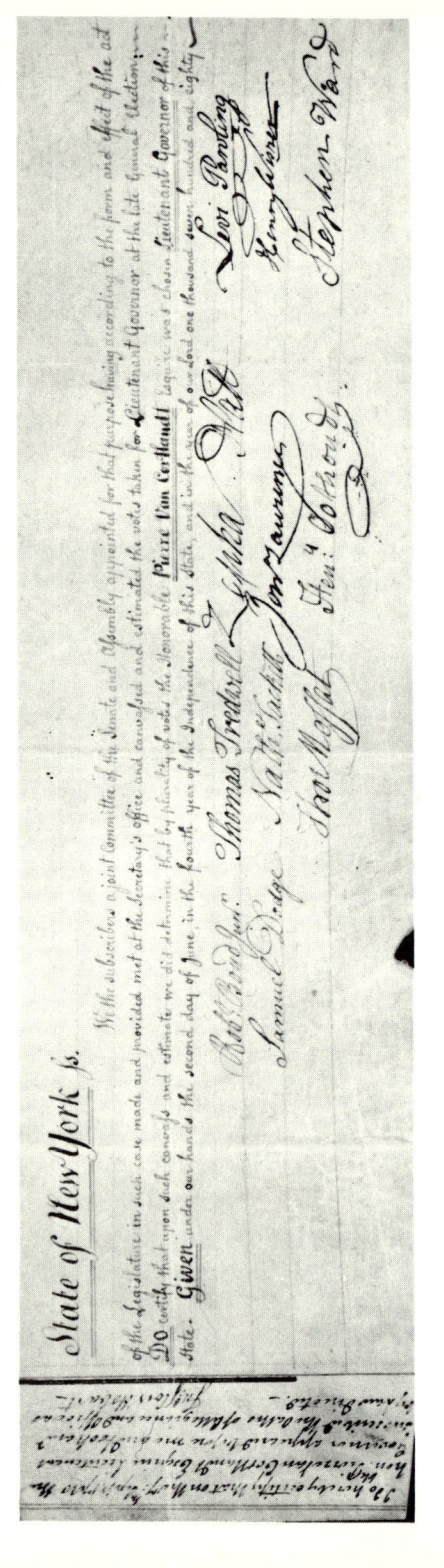

State of New York ss.

We the subscribers a joint Committee of the Senate and Assembly appointed for that purpose having according to the form and effect of the act of the Legislature in such case made and provided met at the Secretary's Office and canvassed and estimated the votes taken for Lieutenant Governor at the late General Election. Do certify that upon such canvass and estimate we did determine that by plurality of votes the Honorable Pierre Van Cortlandt Esquire was chosen Lieutenant Governor of this state. Given under our hands the second day of June, in the fourth year of the Independence of this state, and in the year of our Lord one thousand seven hundred and eighty.

Rob.t Benson Jun.r   Thomas Tredwell   [signature]   Pitt
Samuel Dodge   Nath.l Tuthill   Jon Lawrence
     Thos Moffat   Hen.y Oothout

Levi Pawling
Henry Wisner
Stephen Ward

13. The Bethel Methodist Chapel in Croton, built by Pierre Van Cortlandt on a hill near the old Albany Post Road, about a mile north of the manor. Earlier a member of the Church of England, he had been won over by the spread of Methodism in the late eighteenth century.

2. Official ratification of the 1780 election of Pierre Van Cortlandt as Lieutenant Governor of New York State, a post he held for seventeen years (1777–1795).
←

Before the war, the Van Cortlandt women had begun to be interested in Methodism, and it is known that in 1770 the Reverend George Whitefield preached from the porch of the manor house. It may have been this religious development that led Pierre to envisage the manumission of his slaves. A codicil was prepared for his will, allowing for such a possibility after his death. And as a result his heirs granted their freedom to the remaining slaves: Ishmael, a renowned local fiddler, his wife and daughter, and two other female adults and one child.

Joanna Van Cortlandt died at the manor house in Croton in 1808, and Pierre died there six years later, at the age of ninety-three. At the time, Philip was living there, as were his widowed sister Catharine Van Wyck and her three sons.

When the Town of Cortlandt was established as an administrative unit under the State Constitution, Philip became its first Supervisor. He was a State Assemblyman from 1788 to 1790, and a State Senator from 1791 to 1793. Then he was elected to Congress, where he served for sixteen years. Membership in the House of Representatives, beginning with the Third Congress of the United States, was the highest office he was ever to hold. He served largely on committees of the Congress concerned with military affairs.

However, his first important appointment came in February 1794, when he was named to the committee investigating the Treasury Department. This was a sensitive issue, for it represented Congress's attempt to assert a right of control over the Treasury, in defiance of the one-man rule Alexander Hamilton had set up in it. Having been elected as a Federalist supporter, Philip soon joined Thomas Jefferson and James Madison in the opposition group.

His last vote was cast on March 3, 1809, against the Embargo Act, and he must have been greatly gratified when the House came out 81 to 40 in favor of lifting the embargo.

Retiring at sixty, he kept in close contact with events in Washington through his reading and through his brother Pierre, Jr., who served in the Eleventh and Twelfth Congresses. When James Madison was pitted against DeWitt Clinton in the election of 1812, Philip supported Clinton, due to their close associations as fellow New Yorkers.

In 1824, when the Marquis de Lafayette returned to visit the United States, Philip was one of those who greeted and spent time with him, to share old memories of the war in which together they had helped the new country to be born.

Philip built flour mills on both sides of the Croton River and operated sawmills and a brickyard (Illus. 14). He is also thought to have added a wing to the manor house about 1810.

14. Painting of a mill on the Croton, canvas by an unknown artist (c. 1840), now hanging in the east chamber of the manor house and traditionally considered to be a picture of one of the mills owned by the Van Cortlandt family.

Philip's nephew, Philip G. Van Wyck, son of his sister Catharine, remained in charge at the manor house after his uncle's death in 1831, until 1836 when Pierre Van Cortlandt III (1815–1884), the son of Philip's younger brother Pierre, Jr., came of age and assumed the ownership conveyed to him in Philip's will. In the same year, he married Catharine Elizabeth Beck, of Albany.

This new generation of Van Cortlandts was apparently interested in the topography of the property, for two instructive maps were drawn at about this time. One, done by George W. Cartwright in October 1837, shows the house, barns, ice house, and ferry house, and the ferry route, the Post Road, the pilings of an early bridge, as well as the Quaker Bridge, the family cemetery, and the Methodist Church (Bethel Chapel) (Illus. 13, 15). The other, unsigned, but dated February 19, 1838, displays the buildings themselves in greater detail. The manor house can be seen, with its three porches and a wing on the right (Illus. 16). Around 1845, Pierre III added a west wing to the house, enlarged the east wing, and probably built dormers across the front of the house.

With Catharine's death in 1895, the property passed to their three remaining children, Catherine, James, and Anne. James died in 1917, a bachelor and the last male lineal descendant of the family. Anne also died unmarried, in 1941, and all of the property went to Catherine's two daughters.

In 1945, for the first time since the granting of the Royal Patent of 1697, the manor house was finally sold to a new owner outside the Van Cortlandt family. By now, it stood on only five remaining acres.

It changed ownership several times in rapid succession, until in 1953 John D. Rockefeller, Jr., bought it and concerned himself with seeing that it was restored to its historical appearance and significance.

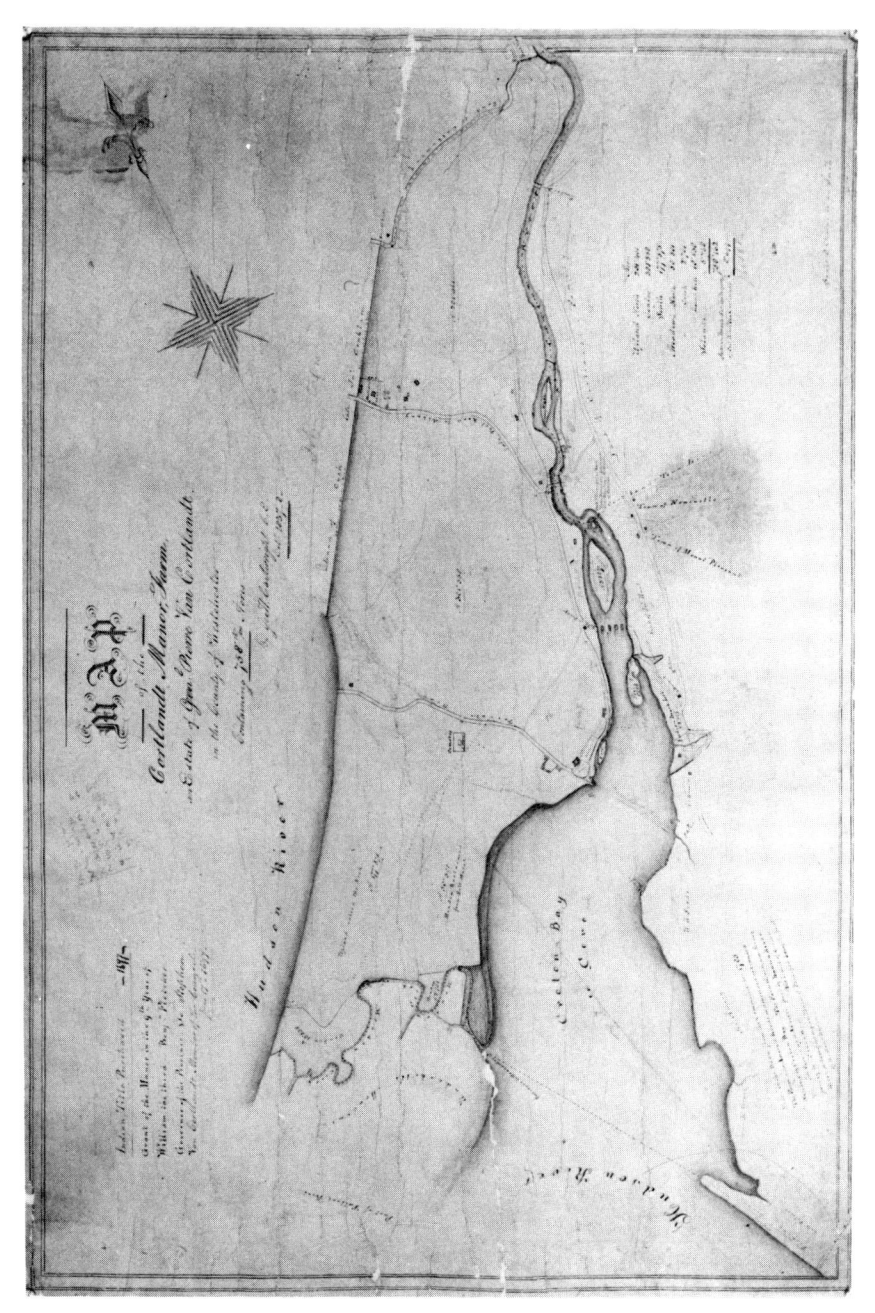

15. Pierre Van Cortlandt III in October 1837 commissioned George W. Cartwright to map the property he had recently inherited; this map shows the major buildings, roads, and bridges near the manor house.

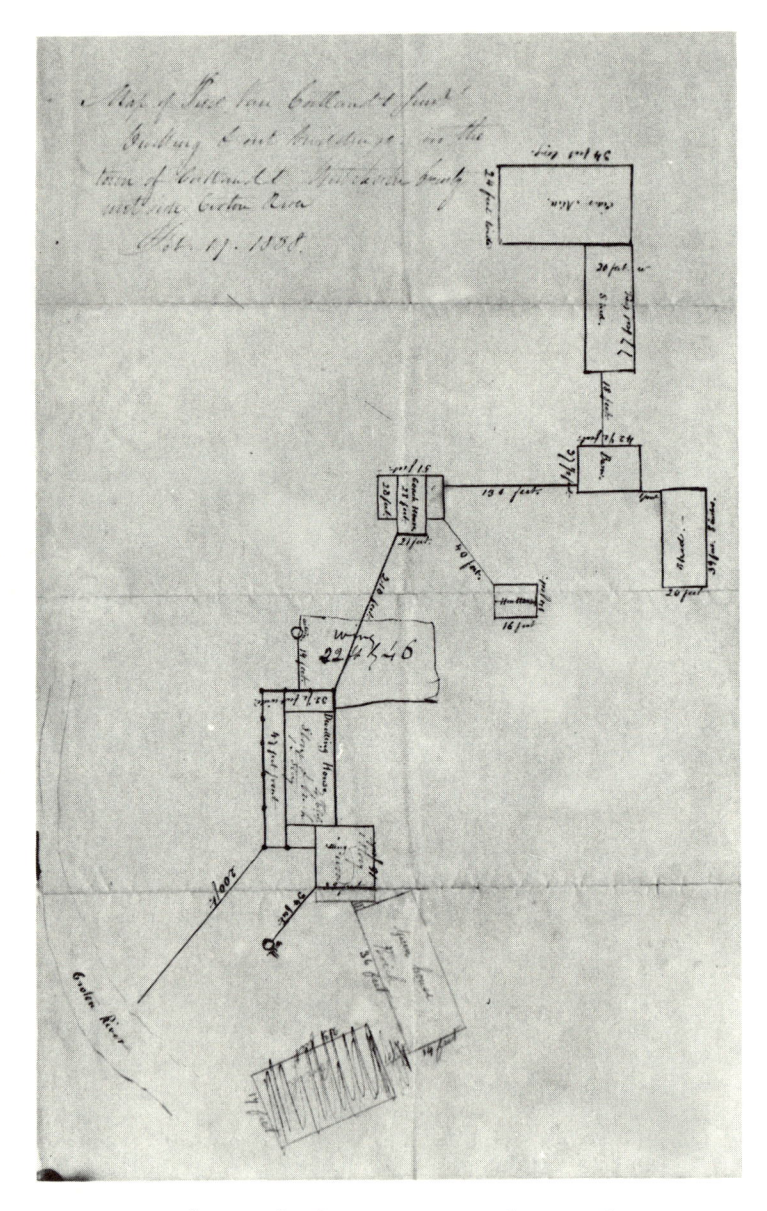

16. Unsigned map of Febrary 19, 1838, showing the manor house in great detail. It can here be clearly seen that the manor house had porches on three sides as well as a wing when this was executed.

The Restoration

AS EARLY AS 1940, five years before the sale of much of the land by the Van Cortlandts, John D. Rockefeller, Jr., had been approached about acquiring the property. Since he had previously made possible the conservation of Philipsburg Manor, Upper Mills, and Washington Irving's home, Sunnyside, both located south of Croton, it was natural that he be considered for such a purchase. But, despite repeated offers over more than a decade, it was not until 1953 that he accepted. The town of Croton had by then been petitioned for a zoning change, which would have resulted in eventual breakup and subdivision of the tract—and this he wished to avoid.

17. Old photograph showing the manor house sometime prior to 1890, after the second wing had been added. Original shape of the roofline remains, but dormers have now been added. The photograph is from the Slater Collection, Ossining, New York.

On June 2, 1953, Mr. Rockefeller effected the purchase of the Van Cortlandt property, including the manor house and five acres of land, so it might be kept intact and turned over to some appropriate organization or agency for future handling. Because of his association with the restoration of Colonial Williamsburg, the eighteenth-century town in Virginia, Mr. Rockefeller turned to the architectural staff of that project for guidance and advice.

Research—architectural, archaeological, and historical—was entrusted to specialists, and they set about acquiring the pertinent documents still in the hands of Van Cortlandt descendants and those owned by other private individuals, to supplement the material available in libraries, archives, or other sources. From all this gradually emerged an increasingly precise picture of the eighteenth-century appearance of the manor.

When the property was acquired in 1953, the manor house consisted of its seventeenth- and eighteenth-century core, plus the two wings that had been added in the nineteenth century (Illus. 17). Lengthy discussions ensued on the question: Should the house be preserved as it now stood or restored to the appearance it had had in the eighteenth century? After the numerous arguments had been considered from all viewpoints, the decision was made to restore the house to the period of the family's greatest political prominence in the state and nation—the period of 1749–1814, dating from the start of Pierre's occupancy until his death.

What the structure looked like in 1783 could be extrapolated from a document written by Pierre and labeled "House and farm at Croton, Losses during the Revolution," which detailed the damage done to the manor house and outbuildings by and through the hostilities (Illus. 18, 19, 20). In 1954, a small amount of additional acreage was acquired, to supplement the reduced five-acre plot on which the

18. View of south elevation of the manor house, showing work on the roof and excavation for brownstone plinths for the porch columns.

19. Another view of south elevation (1955), showing both chimneys complete and new window frames being installed.

20. Photograph (1955) showing filling-in between original shingle strips on south side of the manor house roof.

manor house stood, and negotiations were begun with a view to adding to this the ferry house, now considered an integral part of the project.

By the end of 1954, the ferry house and the frontage on the Croton River had been bought, and in another twelve months plans for the restoration of the property were virtually complete. It was decided that the "Long Walk" between the manor house and the ferry house would be reconstructed, and the gardens extended so as to return them to their original size (Illus. 21). The manor property now had been increased to 125 acres.

The office that Pierre had had erected to the east of the manor house was to be built once again, on its original foundations, brought to light by the archaeologists working on the restoration. Further reconstruction was also to take place on the foundations of the ice house, the necessary house, and the smoke house. By late 1956, this had all been

22. Photograph (1956) showing removal of a nineteenth-century addition and bracing which had been added to the north side of the ferry house.

21. The long walk between manor house and ferry house, as it was reconstructed in brick. Spring flowers blossom in the plots bordering it.

done, and the exterior restoration of the manor house proper was complete.

A foundation unearthed to the west of the ferry house was conjectured to be that of a separate kitchen house. Extensive research was carried out to determine what appearance such a kitchen might have had, and it was eventually re-created in brick, which had been decided upon as the proper material. The architects conformed the building to the style of the Van Alen house at Kinderhook, New York, and other seventeenth-century Dutch structures. There had also been a stable or barn in the area, investigation revealed, but this was not deemed essential to the project at that time.

Obviously, the exterior reconstruction would have been only a sort of false front, if the interior had not been furnished in keeping with it. But most of the important contents of the manor house had been sold off at auctions in 1941 and 1942. By a fortunate twist of fate, it happened that at that time Mr. Rockefeller had acquired a significant nucleus of them to be used as the furnishings for Philipsburg Manor. By special arrangement, it was possible to have these brought back where they had come from, and a careful search was undertaken by the Williamsburg curatorial staff to locate the rest of the original furnishings. Many of them were located and a number found their way back to the manor house, either by purchase or through the generosity of their current owners. The interior of the manor house began to assume much the appearance it had had in the period before all of these items had been dispersed.

As early as 1955, work had begun on the ferry house (Illus. 22), and by 1957 the restoration of this building and its kitchen house had been completed. The landing at the base of the hill in front of them was also in the process of reconstruction (Illus. 23.). But, as the ferry house had been occupied by tenants, none of the original furniture remained in it. Consequently, it was felt that ferry house and kitchen

23. Restored ferry house and reconstructed kitchen house as they looked by 1957, when work on them had been completed. Both buildings face south toward the Croton River and the crossing at the base of the bank before them.

might best serve as an exhibition area for displays of the typical country artifacts of the Hudson River area.

Mr. Rockefeller in 1956 reached the conclusion that the completely restored Van Cortlandt Manor properly belonged in the charge of Sleepy Hollow Restorations, the corporation set up to administer Philipsburg Manor, Upper Mills, and Sunnyside. The transfer of title was made in 1959, and in June of that year the property was opened to the public.

One of the unique assets of Van Cortlandt Manor is thus that it today affords the possibility of seeing preservation, restoration, and reconstruction, all on one original site. The three processes have been combined here to create a setting and atmosphere that takes the visitor back to the period of the property's highest point of development.

A costumed interpreter greets visitors outside the manor house.

Van Cortlandt Manor House, Croton-on-Hudson, New York.

The Manor House

We do not know for certain whether any house stood on the property when the manor was created in 1697. If there was one, possibly on the present site of the manor house, sometime between 1700 and 1748 it became part of the foundation, ground floor, and lower structure of a larger house with walls of red sandstone, red brick, and small yellow Dutch bricks. These walls had small square holes edged with the red brick, leaving narrow slit openings, probably for ventilation when furs and food were stored in the building. Other holes between the windows on all four walls on the main-floor level are typical putlog holes, used for the support of scaffolding.

Nor do we know exactly when there was added a second story, bringing the stone walls to their present height. Some evidence suggests the two-story porch running around three sides was put up at the same time. The roof, prior to 1749, was gabled and, in the Dutch tradition, swept out over the porches at a flatter pitch. In the middle of the eighteenth century, when Pierre was remodeling the house, the north wall was raised about four feet to increase the space in the top story. The roof was also made higher by continuing the slope to a new ridge back toward the north wall. This altered the pitch of the rear roofline, throwing the ridge off balance and creating the roofline that exists today.

When Pierre moved to Croton in 1749 he effected certain improvements: The house now was to have four rooms on the main floor, with bedrooms above, and a commodious kitchen, storage room, and "old parlor" below. Yet the house remained striking in both its architectural and interior simplicity. It is nothing so much as a farmhouse, by contrast with some of the grander manor houses erected at the same period.

As an example, at almost exactly the same time (1748), Frederick Van Cortlandt was building a house for himself in what is today Van Cortlandt Park, in the Bronx. Frederick was the son of Jacobus Van Cortlandt, youngest son of Oloff, and thus Pierre's first cousin once removed. Frederick's house is far more imposing, a pure statement of Georgian architecture. It survives as a two-story stone building with window key blocks carved in the shape of actors' masks. However, the paneling of the interiors of the two houses bear marked resemblances, so that the interior in the case of the Bronx house is much simpler than its exterior.

In order to discuss the individual rooms of the manor house, we must clarify what our references to "original objects" among the furnishings will mean.

During the Revolution, it will be recalled, Pierre

moved his family first to Peekskill, then to Rhinebeck. Lists of furniture and other household goods were made at this time, and until 1836 the Van Cortlandts maintained both Croton and Peekskill houses. Pierre's son, Pierre, Jr., who was married twice, furnished the Peekskill house and lived there. The widowed daughter of Pierre I, Catharine (Mrs. Abraham Van Wyck), and his eldest son, General Philip Van Cortlandt, a bachelor, lived in the Croton house. Philip looked on his sister Catharine's son, Philip G. Van Wyck, named for him, as his own adopted son, and gave him the furnishings of the Croton house, as well as the freedom to live there until Pierre III, son of his brother Pierre, Jr., should come of age in 1836.

In view of this, Philip G. Van Wyck in 1835 moved to a new house, Grove Hill, in the nearby village of Sing-Sing, taking with him the Croton house furniture, some of which dated back to the time of his grandfather, Pierre.

24. The manor house as it appeared in the 1848 edition of Robert Bolton's *History of the County of Westchester*, in a woodcut by Frederick A. Chapman (1818–1891), who was a portrait, historical, and landscape painter, and engraver, as well as a designer of stained glass.

When Pierre III married Albany-born Catharine Beck, they occupied the Croton house (Illus. 24). They brought with them furnishings from the Peekskill house as well as furniture, silver, ceramics, and portraits belonging to the Beck family and others among her relatives, the Caldwells and Romeyns. These included a writing table at which DeWitt Clinton had been sitting when he died, and portraits painted about 1720 of Caleb Beck of Schenectady, and his wife, the former Annetje Mabie Fairley. Important pieces of silver by Isaac Hutton, G. Hall, and other famed silversmiths came to the manor house in this way, as did part of the Chinese export porcelain that had been brought from China to James Caldwell, John Stevenson, and Pierre Van Cortlandt. At his father's death in 1848, Pierre III inherited his entire estate, and the Peekskill furnishings thus more than took the place of what Philip had bequeathed to his namesake.

Of prime importance among the family furnishings are the portraits of three of the children of the first Philip Van Cortlandt and his wife, Catharine DePeyster, Abraham, John, and Pierre, painted about 1730. The portrait of Abraham is now in the Croton manor house while the other two are in the collection of the Brooklyn Museum. A silver teakettle by Cornelius Kierstede, which came to the Van Cortlandts from the DePeysters, is now at the Metropolitan Museum of Art. Portraits painted about 1710 of Philip and Catharine Van Cortlandt were taken to Grove Hill by Philip Van Wyck and remained in the possession of his descendants until around 1940 when they dropped from sight.

So, among "original" furnishings, we now include all of those objects which, through the pattern of intermarriage among the early New York families, came to the manor house—although not all of them were perhaps ever in the manor house at any one time.

The visitor entering the "old parlor" on the lower level is greeted by a sense of intimacy (Illus. 25). The furniture is chiefly of the type made by local joiners in the Hudson River Valley well on into the nineteenth century, although the type of side chair with rush seat seen here is still referred to as "Queen Anne." The antlers of Pierre's pet deer hang on the paneled fireplace wall, along with rifles and powder horns engraved with maps of the Hudson River, in use during the French and Indian War.

25. The "old parlor," a popular room in the eighteenth century, served as both sitting and dining room. The fielded paneling of the fireplace wall is painted tan, the cupboard interiors orange or Dutch red. Furniture ranges in date from late seventeenth to second half of eighteenth century, all of Hudson River Valley origin, chiefly representing the craft of the joiner. The upholstery fabric in the room is resist-dyed linen in pheasant pattern. The early-nineteenth-century still life on the wall belonged to the family.

49

To the left of the fireplace, a commodious cupboard is filled with mid-eighteenth-century delft, most of it English, but some Dutch. To the right, the cupboard contains a collection of various kinds of English pottery. The color combination of orange and putty on the fireplace wall and the blue of the resist-dyed draperies and upholstery lends a rich feeling to the interior.

The kitchen is unique in the great variety of family-owned objects it contains. One of these, the work table below the front windows, was made during the eighteenth century in the Hudson Valley, and traces of its original gray paint can still be detected at its base. Its unusual cross-stretcher system is typical of the area (Illus. 26). Many of the fireplace and cooking implements come from various branches of the Van Cortlandt family, as does the pewter in the slant-front cupboard, by the Spackmans, famous London pewterers.

The milk room to the rear of the kitchen has its original cobbled floor and an imposing cupboard, a family piece that dates from the early eighteenth century and retains its gray paint. This room would have served to store many of the items used in the kitchen, and the two rooms combined present a good picture of domestic life in the 1700s. As they are now used for cooking demonstrations, the rooms heighten the feeling of living history in the home.

A narrow staircase leads to the main floor of the house. Here, a new kind of architectural proportion is in evidence. The front door, massive and double in the Dutch tradition, contains two oval glass openings that allow a small amount of light to filter in, typical of the period. The height of the ceiling and the rich mahogany graining of the woodwork and staircase provide a feeling completely different from that of the floor below. The great black painted armchair behind the front door, made in New York circa 1690–1700, is one of the treasured early family heirlooms. On it hangs a wood panel

26. The unusual type of X-braced base in this table would seem to have been one of the chief characteristics of mid-eighteenth-century Hudson Valley furniture. Wear has removed the original paint from the top of this piece, but the brace still retains traces of the type of gray paint contemporary travelers mention as typical of the Valley.

painted with the Van Cortlandt coat of arms, signed by G. Kane. The portrait of Abraham in its original frame hangs over a Hudson River Valley blanket chest.

The side chair with caned back and seat (from about 1700) belonged to Kiliaen Van Rensselaer, a great-grandson of Oloff Van Cortlandt, thus Pierre I's third cousin (Illus. 27). The half-round mahogany table in the rear hall (c. 1790) with the label of a New York cabinetmaker, Elbert Anderson, came to the manor through Catharine Elizabeth Beck Van Cortlandt, who inherited it from her maternal grandfather, James Caldwell (Illus. 28). Here, too, is the portrait of Joanna Livingston, who married Pierre I in 1748, painted by Ezra Ames (1768–1836), an important portraitist of New York families.

The parlor to the right of the front door, probably the most elegant room in the house (Illus. 29), is the room in which, according to family tradition, Benjamin Franklin spent a night late in May 1776, en route back from an unsuccessful mission to Canada. Both this room and the "old parlor" below may have done double duty as both parlors and living accommodations.

Here the paneled fireplace wall is painted gray, with a cupboard interior of orange. Though we can only speculate, it is thought that the walls date from the mid-1700s and that the fireplaces were replaced about 1805, in the then-popular neoclassical style. The furniture ranges from Queen Anne and Chippendale to neoclassical, or over a period from about 1740 to the start of the next century. As in the other rooms, furnishings are arranged to illustrate a way of life, rather than to represent a perfect "period" decor. The use of the venetian blinds is based on their specific listing in an inventory made by General Philip.

One of the blanc-de-chine figures on the mantel belonged to the family, as did the flat-top secretary bookcase in the Chippendale style (Illus. 30). A Queen Anne wing chair

27. Entrance-hall woodwork is grained in dark red-brown, to simulate the rich color of mahogany. The portrait of Abraham Van Cortlandt from about 1720 (Illus. 4) hangs above a blanket chest of local origin. The chest rests on its original turned bulbous feet. The ebonized William and Mary side chair with cane back and seat comes from Rensselaerswyck, near Albany.

28. Two signed pieces of furniture are in the rear hall. The classical table bears the branded name of Elbert Anderson, who worked in New York City in the 1790s; it came to the manor house through Catharine Elizabeth Beck Van Cortlandt. The looking-glass is labeled by Delvecchio, also active in New York at about the same time. The small framed drawing by an unknown artist of the late eighteenth century is thought to be of Gilbert Van Cortlandt (1757–1786).

29. The most elegant room of the house is the parlor on the main floor, with its gray-painted fielded paneling and orange or Dutch red cupboard interior. The mantelpiece, replaced in about 1805 in the then-popular neoclassical style, is more recent than the fireplace wall, and furnishings of the room range from the Queen Anne to the neoclassical periods. The Queen Anne table is a well-documented family possession, as are the side chairs used with it. The camelback sofa is New York Chippendale. The portraits hanging over it, of Captain and Mrs. Caleb Beck (from about 1720–1733) are by an unknown artist. This room contains a large selection of Chinese export porcelain. The French mantel clock (c. 1809) is the most recent object in the room.

55

of about 1740, included here, belonged to Philip Van Wyck, who had inherited it from Philip Van Rensselaer. Particularly noteworthy is the portrait of Pierre I by John Wesley Jarvis (1780–1840) painted about 1810, when the subject was in his late eighties. The cupboard to the left of the fireplace is filled with fine specimens of Chinese export porcelain, all from the last half of the eighteenth century or the first years of the nineteenth. The latest object in the room is the French clock, purchased in New York in 1809 by Pierre, Jr., at a cost of $170.

The fireplace wall of the dining room has the same type of paneling as the parlor and an identical mantelpiece with the same paint colors (Illus. 31). The dominant piece of furniture here is the massive drop-leaf table with mahogany top, from the turn of the eighteenth century (Illus. 32). This and one other example document the first use of mahogany in American furniture; locally obtained cherry was used for the table base, and poplar is the secondary wood. This is certainly the table mentioned in the list of objects moved to Peekskill by Pierre I. The late-eighteenth-century neoclassical New York sideboard belonged to Pierre, Jr., who also owned the English knifeboxes placed on it (Illus. 33). The Chippendale pier looking-glass hangs over a Chippendale slab-top mixing table, and the latest piece of furniture here is the serving table between the windows at the front; it is New York neoclassical, dating from about 1810. Pieces of family silver are also included here (Illus. 34).

The ceramics are particularly worthy of note. The porcelain figures on the mantel, three from the Chelsea factory and two from the Chelsea-Derby factory, represent Mercury, Minerva, Diana, Milton, and Shakespeare. These belonged to Cornelia Van Cortlandt Beekman and were probably used at both Croton and Philipsburg Manor, Upper Mills, in North Tarrytown, which she purchased as a home in 1785 (Illus. 35). The Chinese export and Canton porcelain in the

30. Early-eighteenth-century Tê-hua (blanc de chine) porcelain group of a European couple seated on a Fo, with smaller figures below. Often mentioned in late-nineteenth- and early-twentieth-century sources about the manor house, this figure returned to it as a bequest of Miss Charlotte Van Cortlandt. It is an unusually fine specimen of this kind of porcelain to be found in this country.

31. The dining room on the opposite side of the house has the same fireplace-wall treatment and color as the parlor. Its mantelpiece has a group of Chelsea and Chelsea-Derby figurines; made in England around 1760, two of them represent Shakespeare and Milton, the others Minerva, Mercury, and Diana. Once the property of Cornelia Van Cortlandt Beekman, they were probably used at both the manor house and Philipsburg Manor, Upper Mills, North Tarrytown. The cupboard contains a variety of Chinese export porcelain and Canton, all of which belonged to the family. A long painted and gilded yellow pine pier mirror hangs over the slab-top mixing table; both of these pieces date from the mid-eighteenth century and were made in New York.

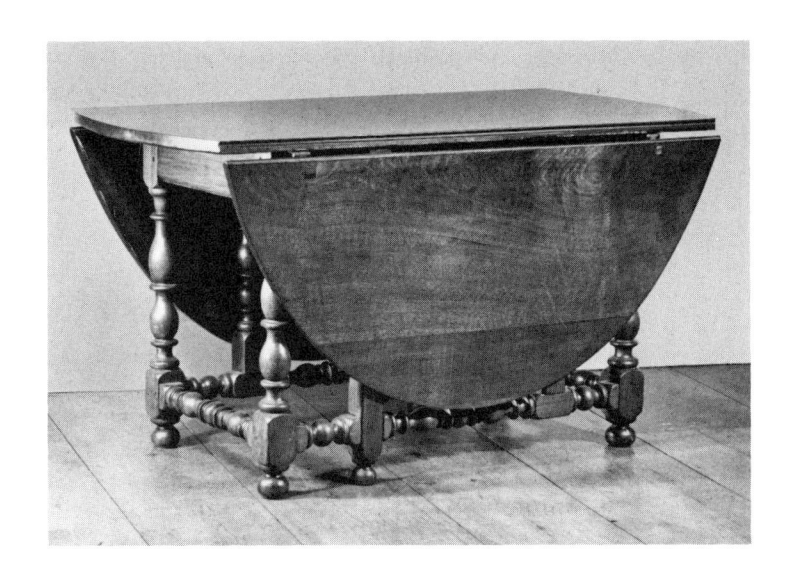

32. This family-owned table is of particular interest, as its top records the early American use of mahogany. Dating from the late seventeenth century or early eighteenth century, it is probably from the Hudson Valley. Its style is William and Mary, with turned legs and gates that can support rounded drop leaves; the legs are cherry and the secondary wood is poplar.

33. New York City sideboard (from about 1790–1800), a family piece made of mahogany inlaid with husks in a lighter wood. Interestingly, when this was reproduced in Harold D. Eberlein's *The Manors and Historic Houses of the Hudson Valley* (1924), it occupied the same position in the dining room as it does today.

34. One of the few pieces of original manor house silver not in other collections, this coffeepot was made in London by William and R. Peaston, 1762–1763. Engraved with the script initials AS, for Ann Stevenson, it came into the family when she married Pierre Van Cortlandt, Jr., in 1813.

61

35. Ivory miniature of Cornelia (1753–1847), third child of Pierre and Joanna Livingston Van Cortlandt, who became Mrs. Gerard G. Beekman, Jr., in 1769. In 1785, the Beekmans purchased the property now known as Philipsburg Manor, Upper Mills, in North Tarrytown. Painted in her later years by an artist unknown, this miniature belongs to Mrs. Edward Crary Cammann. The photo is from the Frick Art Reference Library.

cupboard to the left of the fireplace is part of what came from the Becks, the Caldwells, and the Stevensons.

The portraits here of Pierre, Jr., and his wife, Ann Stevenson, in their original frames, were painted in Albany by Ezra Ames around 1815 (Illus. 36, 37). The lace mitts worn by Ann in the portrait are now in the manor house collection (Illus. 38).

The door to the right in the rear hall leads to the northeast bed chamber. The paneled wall here is like those of the parlor and dining room, but there is no mantel. The paneling is painted and grained a rich dark-mahogany color. The earliest piece is the English Queen Anne armchair, one of the very few non-New York items of furniture in the house. The elaborate New York Chippendale chest-on-chest and the bed also come from the family. At one point in the year, generally during the winter, the bed is hung with late-eighteenth-century English copperplate-printed hangings which belonged in the manor house. The stove of the same period was found in the house at the time of the restoration (Illus. 40). Over the fireplace opening hangs a painting by an unknown artist: a mill on the Croton, generally considered to be one of the Van Cortlandt mills.

The room on the other side of the hall has traditionally been known as the Prophet's Chamber (Illus. 41). It gets its name from the many Methodist preachers who slept in it during the late eighteenth and the nineteenth centuries. A mezzotint of the Rev. George Whitefield hangs here as a reminder of this.

The fireplace wall is similar to that of the northeast chamber, but it is painted an orange-red color. The initials carved in it are unexplained. Another non-New York piece is seen here: the dressing table in Chippendale style, made in Philadelphia, which belonged to Cornelia Van Cortlandt Beekman (Illus. 42). The inlaid firescreen, or ladies', desk, of neoclassical style (c. 1785), belonged to Ann Stevenson

36. Pierre Van Cortlandt, Jr., (1762–1848), painted in Albany by Ezra Ames, about 1816. He married his second wife, Ann Stevenson, in 1813, and this and a companion painting of her were executed at the same time. The portraits reverted to Van Cortlandt Manor in 1848 after the death of Pierre, who had lived his adult life in Albany and Peekskill.

37. Ann Stevenson Van Cortlandt (1774–1821), in the companion portrait to Illustration 36; this is undoubtedly the painting referred to in a receipt in the Sleepy Hollow Restorations collection dated December 15, 1815, Albany, and signed "E. Ames." Made out to Pierre Van Cortlandt, it is for a portrait of "his lady" ($35) and a burnished gilt frame ($25). Both portraits are in their original gilt neoclassical frames.

38. The lace mitts Ann Stevenson Van Cortlandt was wearing when the Ames portrait was painted. They were made about 1815, either in England or in America.

39. The northeast bedchamber contains an imposing Chippendale chest-on-chest (c. 1765), which descended in the family. The paneled wall here is grained to simulate a very dark mahogany. The marbleized floor used in the parlor is based on remnants of the original treatment found in the small closet space between this room and the parlor at the front of the house. One of the few English pieces of furniture is the Queen Anne walnut armchair. During the winter, the bed is hung with its original eighteenth-century copperplate-printed cotton curtains, made in England.

40. Cast iron stove, probably made in New York City in late 1700s. Found at the time of the restoration walled within the fireplace, it had been shown in many early-twentieth-century photographs of the interior of the manor house.

41. The Prophet's Chamber, so called because many of the visiting Methodist leaders and preachers slept here. The fireplace wall has orange-red paint, with unexplained initials carved into the paneling. As in the northeast chamber, the original hangings are used on the bed in the winter months.

42. This mahogany dressing table, made about 1750–1770, is the only piece of Philadelphia furniture in the family collection. It belonged to Cornelia Van Cortlandt Beekman, and was probably used both at Croton and at Philipsburg Manor, Upper Mills, as were the figurines in the dining room (Illus. 31).

Van Cortlandt (Illus. 43). The Chippendale corner or toilet chair came from John Stevenson, Ann's father (Illus. 44). Again, during the winter, a rare set of English copperplate-printed cotton bed hangings, from the house, are used here; few American houses can boast such documented textiles (Illus. 45).

The top floor is reached by a two-part mahogany-grained staircase, leading to a spacious hall. A mahogany Chippendale press cupboard, representative of the full development of this style in New York case furniture, stands here (Illus. 46), and a set of chairs in neoclassical taste are placed about the area. The top floor also served as sleeping quarters for family members, particularly the children.

A bedroom on the east side contains a low-post bed and numerous articles of family furniture. Important among them are a simple Chippendale fall-front desk and neoclassical Pembroke table (Illus. 47). The lean-to room at the rear is furnished with several low-post and children's beds. In all likelihood the arrangement of these rooms was very informal, with pallets sometimes spread on the floor for sleeping, since this was a general custom at the time.

The rich manor house collection of highly documented original materials was made possible only through the research and investigation carried out at the time of the restoration, and the generous cooperation of descendants of the Van Cortlandt family. The latter agreed to part with treasured heirlooms so that they might be returned to their ancestral manor house and its documentation thus be made more complete for the visitor of today.

43. Firescreen (or ladies') desk, made of mahogany and inlaid with exotic woods and brass, probably made in New York City around 1785. This rare form in American furniture belonged to Ann Stevenson Van Cortlandt, second wife of Pierre, Jr., and was used as an illustration in Esther Singleton's *The Furniture of Our Forefathers* (1901).

44. Corner chair of mahogany, with pine as secondary wood, probably from New York City (c. 1765). Originally owned by John Stevenson (father-in-law of Pierre Van Cortlandt, Jr.), it was conceived as a toilet chair, but the toilet compartment has since been removed.

45. New England post-bed in the Prophet's Chamber, shown hung with the original set of copperplate-printed cotton made in England in the late 1700s.

46. This massive linen press of mahogany was probably made in New York City in 1770. It has an imposing place at the top of the stairs leading to the third floor. The carved fretwork under the cornice and chamfered edges with lambs' tongues are typical of New York cabinetmaking of this period. It is one of the documented pieces from the manor house.

47. Representative of the simple type of family furniture in the manor house is this Pembroke table of curly maple, probably made in New York State about 1800. It came from the Caldwell family, ancestors of Catharine Elizabeth Beck Van Cortlandt, wife of Pierre III.

48. The bronze ferry bell at the top of the steep drive up from the landing, dated 1799. It was probably used to summon the ferry from across the Croton.

Ferry house (above) and kitchen house (below), showing the ferrymaster's bell.

The Ferry House
and Kitchen House

At the opposite end of the "Long Walk" from the manor house stands the restored ferry house and its adjacent reconstructed kitchen house. Before the ferry house is the landing for the ferry across the Croton River used by Albany Post Road travelers between Albany and New York City. At the top of the hill from the landing is the old bronze bell once located on the south side of the river, where it served to summon the ferry (Illus. 48).

The ferry house is a one-and-a-half-story brick-and-timber building with two chimneys. It was already there when Pierre inherited the property in 1748. Its interior is arranged in a four-room central hall plan, which would appear to have been developed later in the eighteenth century.

The building was leased to a long series of tenants who lived there and operated the tavern and ferry. No inventories of any of these tenants have ever come to light. So, at the time of restoration, it was decided that the building and its kitchen should be used to house a collection of furnishings such as might have been used by the tenants, things that are simpler and of a more local nature than those to be found in the manor house.

Entry to the ferry house is through a small entrance hall. The rates of ferriage would most certainly have been posted here, and we have a list of them, as signed in 1792 by General Philip Van Cortlandt. It reads:

Rate of Ferrage, from the first day of May
to the first day of November for a man and
Horse–4^d: a One Horse Sulkey or Chair. 1/.
a Waggon with 2 Horses and Load – 2/–
a Cart and Oxen ~~with or Without Horses~~ 2/
a Pheaton and pair ——————————— 2/
all four wheal Carriages with 2. Horses. 2/ ⎫ Chariots.
if four Horses the Carriage   3/ ⎭ or Coaches –
foot Passingers—2^d—

from the first of November to the first of
May the ferrage of a man and horse to
be. 6^d: but no alteration as to any other
Unless to Carry a foot Passenger to the
foot of the hill which is at all times to
be four Pence———given under my
Hand May. 1. 1792
                  Ph. V. Cortlandt[5]
[Endorsed] Rate of Ferrage
      1792=

The entrance hall has a slant-front desk-on-frame in which a register of lodgers would probably have been kept. Throughout this building, the walls are whitewashed and the trim painted a gray tan.

The common room was once part of a single room that extended the full length of the house (Illus. 49). The fireplace is a nineteenth-century replacement of a much larger one, originally in the corner. People waiting for the ferry could gather here to talk, eat, and drink, as in any modern depot or passenger station. Committees of neighborhood organizations also met here on a regular basis, and it was a

49. Common room of the ferry house, to the left of the entrance hall, furnished as such a room might have been for eating, drinking, and general relaxation. Furniture here is all typical of local Hudson River Valley products of the second half of the eighteenth century. Ceramics, imported chiefly from England, are representative of such items, including yellow ware, scratched ware, and delft.

regular stop for cattle drovers, notorious carriers of gossip through the countryside.

The table at the center of the room has a top which can be shifted on a dowel so as to convert it into a chair and storage piece (Illus. 50), a local product, made in the Hudson Valley around 1750. Surrounding it are country Queen Anne chairs with rush seats and variations on the pad or disc foot (Illus. 51). The painted kas (or Dutch cupboard) to the right of the fireplace is an unusual item, as only a small number in this form with painted decoration survive today (Illus. 52). They were made at the turn of the eighteenth century in the Hudson Valley. The corner cupboard with orange-painted interior and hanging shelf houses a collection of eighteenth-century English pottery.

Behind this room is the barroom. The bar itself is a reconstruction (Illus. 53). An even larger convertible-top table is seen here, combining the same features of seat and storage furniture as the one in the common room. The table is surrounded by Windsor chairs from Kingston, New York, dating from the last quarter of the eighteenth century. The red-painted pewter dresser against the far wall was found in the Albany area, in the neighborhood of Rensselaerswyck (Illus. 54). The dresser is furnished with a collection of English and American pewter, the latter made in Rhode Island, Massachusetts, Connecticut, Philadelphia, and New York, while the bar is fitted with bottles, glasses, measures, funnels, and all the other paraphernalia connected with the dispensing of drinks.

The northeast room adjoining the bar is the ferry keeper's room; it is fitted with a built-in or box bed (often called a *slaap banck*) (Illus. 55). This one is reconstructed, based on evidence found in the Abraham Hasbrouck house in New Paltz, New York. A heavy storage piece painted green, seen here, is actually part of an eighteenth-century kas which was later given legs. The two chests in this room

50. Convertibility, an important factor in seventeenth- and eighteenth-century furniture, continued to be so in pieces of a simple country type. This convertible-top table with seat and storage compartment below dates from the Hudson River Valley, circa 1750.

51. A Queen Anne rush-seat turned chair, such as were made in northern New Jersey, Long Island, and the Hudson Valley, from about 1759 into the early 1800s; made by a joiner, it would have been painted by him to cover the variety of different woods employed.

52. The painted kas is a rare form in early-eighteenth-century Hudson Valley crafts. This example exhibits trophies of fruit as well as angels blowing trumpets. Enough of the original decoration still survives to give an idea of the colorful characteristics of the piece. It is on loan from the collection of Mrs. Mitchell Taradash.

53. Barroom of the ferry house with its bar reconstructed after models of several extant mid-eighteenth-century examples. Woodwork is painted gray and again the furniture is of a country type. Various kinds of Windsor chairs surround two convertible-top tables.

54. The pewter cupboard or dresser at the other end of the barroom is decorated with its original red paint; it contains a large display of pewter, both American and English.

55. The ferry keeper's room contains a number of pieces of Hudson Valley country furniture. The blanket chest with two drawers below is of particular interest for the fine example of primitive painting which decorates its front. The slant-top writing box placed on the table is an early stage in the development of the fall-front desk.

56. The multipurpose parlor of the ferry house served as a general living room as well as a bedroom. Stick turned chairs of about 1700 come from Rensselaerswyck, where they were undoubtedly made by a local joiner. The large fireplace, occupying the entire corner, is probably the type that originally would have been in the common room.

have surfaces decorated in a freehand manner. Three framed anti-British prints hang on the wall—the more historically interesting for having been printed in England for export to the restive colonies.

The southeast room has been furnished as a multipurpose room reserved for ladies (Illus. 56). It might serve as parlor in the daytime and bedroom at night. This, too, was earlier part of the large room that ran east-west across the whole house. A large fireplace with heavy moulded framing occupies the northeast corner of this room. The two large stick-construction armchairs, of the kind that in New England would be called Carver-Brewster type, actually come from New York. Several of these chairs have been found in the vicinity of Beacon and Greene. A heavy kas with bold overhanging cornice is also an important part of the room furnishings.

The upstairs is partitioned: one room on either side of the landing, and a long lean-to or eaves bedroom running the entire length of the rear of the building. Each of the bedrooms has several beds, to be shared by several travelers, as was customarily done in eighteenth-century inns and taverns. The southwest chamber is furnished with three beds, one with a canopy, the others low-post. The southeast chamber has two beds, one of each sort. Another Hudson Valley kas occupies a wall of this room. The north chamber is furnished as an eaves bedroom, with one oak low-post bed. As in the case of the manor house lean-to room, this would probably also have had pallets on the floor.

The ferry kitchen house is designed as a steep-pitched, gable-roofed one-and-a-half-story brick building of one room, with a one-story frame lean-to section across the back. At the east end, the beehive-domed bakeoven is exposed to the exterior, plastered and protected by a shingle roof. It was conjectured that this building was a kitchen house, because the eighteenth-century part of the ferry house did not reveal

57. This reconstructed hooded fireplace in the ferry house kitchen, based on several New York State prototypes, is backed with mid-eighteenth-century Dutch tiles showing children playing games, and has a cast iron fireback. The furniture in this entire building was made in the Hudson River Valley by local joiners and generally dates from the second half of the eighteenth century. There is another convertible-top table in the foreground, and the painted and turned chair to the left of the fireplace is an example of the most robust type of turning that might have been found in such pieces of furniture.

any evidence of a kitchen at that time, and charred remains were found in the excavated foundations on which the kitchen house was reconstructed.

The interior consists of a keeping room or kitchen, the lean-to area, and a large unfinished garret. The floors in this building have been scrubbed with sand, giving them the very clean appearance described by eighteenth-century visitors to the area. A great curtained fireplace hood overhangs the hearth and has a Dutch delft-tiled wall behind it (Illus. 57). The room is now furnished as a multipurpose area, indicated in part by the presence of the box bed or *slaap banck*. The furniture is all of the type made by county joiners in the Hudson Valley. Pewter and ironwork of very fine quality are to be seen here.

The lean-to addition served as a storage and serving area. The food was cooked in the fireplace and then passed through the side door into the barroom of the ferry house. The area contains tables, casks, and a simplified pewter dresser, filled with some large pieces of American and English pewter. By contrasting the country furnishings of these buildings with the elegant furnishings of the manor house, associated with the patrician families who lived in the Hudson Valley during the eighteenth century, one obtains a good perspective on the differences in taste and living accommodations that prevailed in this period from just before to just after the Revolutionary War.

NOTES

1. Philip Van Cortlandt Will, Klapper Library, Queens College, City University of New York.

2. Jacob Judd, ed., *The Revolutionary War Memoir and Selected Correspondence of Philip Van Cortlandt.* Van Cortlandt Family Papers, Vol. 1. (Tarrytown, New York: Sleepy Hollow Restorations, 1976), p. 32.

3. Jacob Judd, ed., *Correspondence of the Van Cortlandt Family of Cortlandt Manor, 1748–1800.* Van Cortlandt Family Papers, Vol. 2. (Tarrytown, New York: Sleepy Hollow Restorations, 1977), pp. 333–334.

4. J. Thomas Scharf, ed., *History of Westchester County, New York.* (Philadelphia, 1886), II, 431.

5. Original document in the collection of Sleepy Hollow Restorations.

Ground Floor

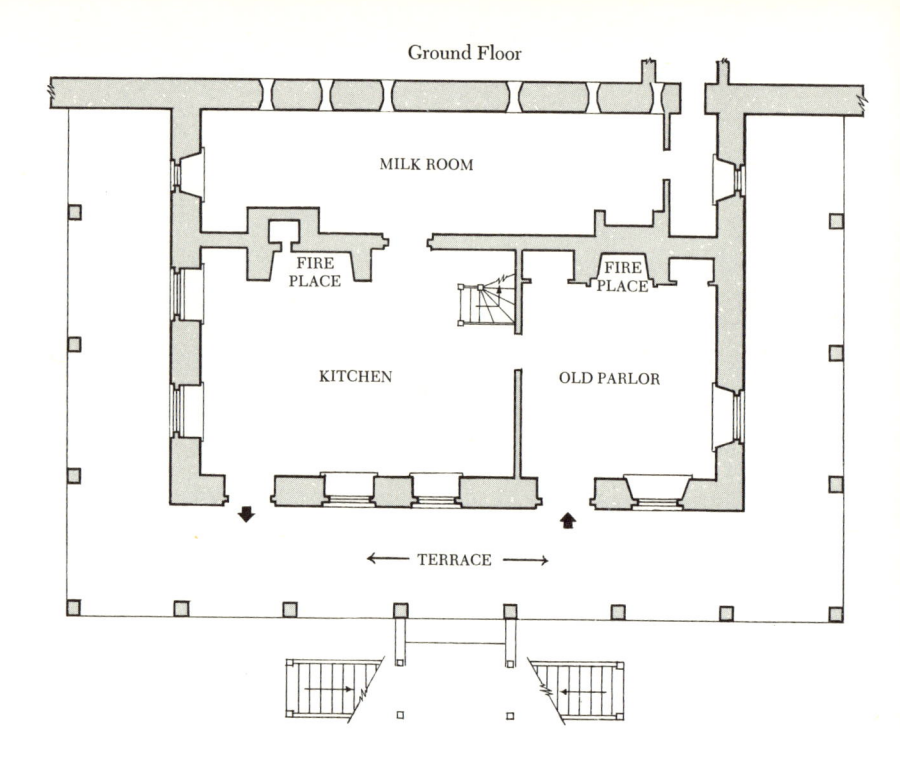

Ground floor plan showing: Milk Room, Kitchen with Fire Place, Old Parlor with Fire Place, and Terrace.

First or Main Floor

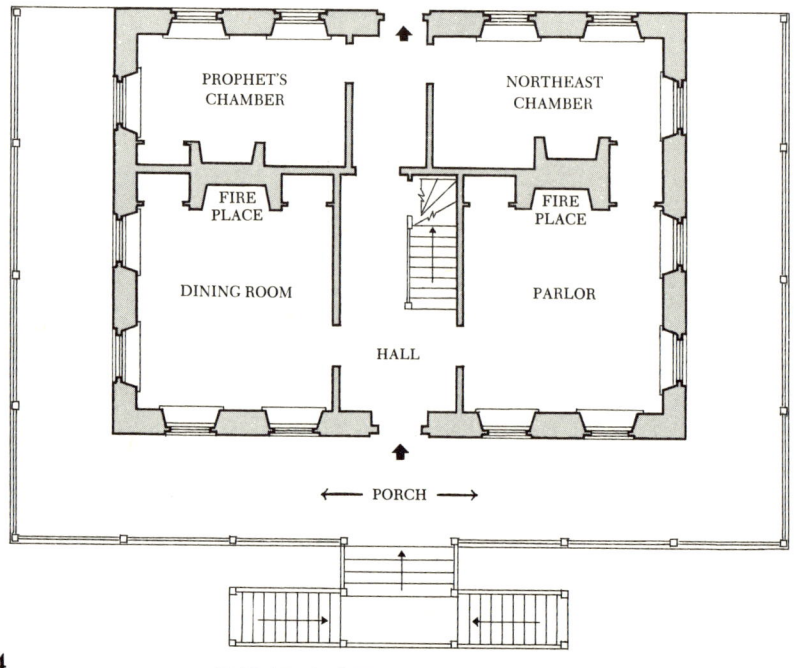

Main floor plan showing: Prophet's Chamber, Northeast Chamber, Dining Room with Fire Place, Parlor with Fire Place, Hall, and Porch.

PLAN OF VAN CORTLANDT MANOR HOUSE

Second or Top Floor

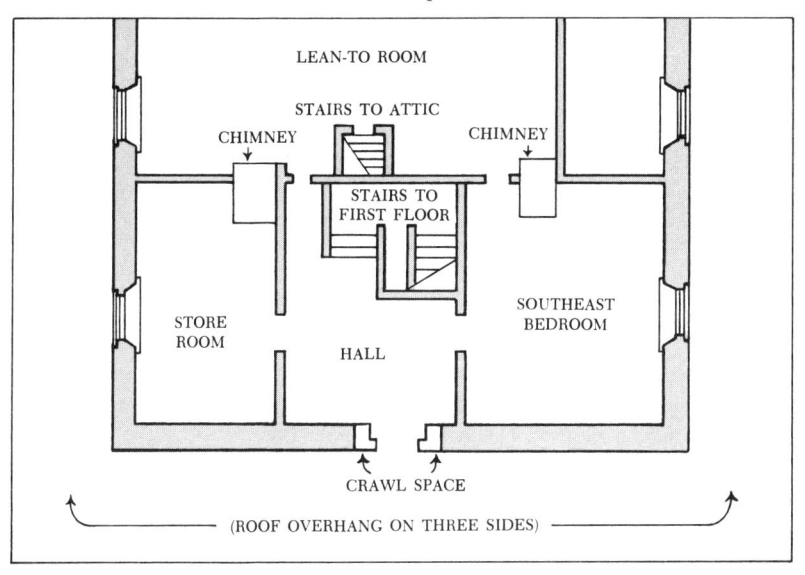

Floor plans of the three levels of the restored Van Cortlandt manor house.

SELECTED BIBLIOGRAPHY

Bolton, Robert. *History of the County of Westchester.* New York, 1848.

Brown, Charles H. *Van Cortlandt Manor.* Tarrytown, New York, 1965.

Butler, Joseph T. *The Family Collections at Van Cortlandt Manor.* Tarrytown, New York, 1967.

Colonial Willamsburg, Architects Office of. *Architectural Record of the Restoration of Van Cortlandt Manor at Croton-on-Hudson, New York for Mr. John D. Rockefeller, Jr.* Mimeographed. Williamsburg, Virginia, May 1, 1959.

Colonial Williamsburg, Architects Office of. *Interpretative Paper of the Restoration of Van Cortlandt Manor at Croton-on-Hudson, New York, for Mr. John D. Rockefeller, Jr.* (Written by Mrs. Antoinette F. Downing, Historian.) Mimeographed. Williamsburg, Virginia, May 1, 1959.

Downing, Antoinette F. *Furnishings Report of the Restorqtion of Van Cortlandt Manor at Croton-on-Hudson, New York for Mr. John D. Rockefeller, Jr.* Mimeographed. Williamsburg, Virginia, 1959.

Eberlein, Harold D. *The Manors and Historic Houses of the Hudson Valley.* Philadelphia, 1924.

Freeman, Robert E. *The Restoration of Van Cortlandt Manor.* Unpublished paper written for Restoration Seminar, Columbia University, 1974–1975. Mimeographed.

Judd, Jacob, ed. *The Revolutionary War Memoir and Selected Correspondence of Philip Van Cortlandt.* Van Cortlandt Family Papers, Vol. 1. Tarrytown, New York, 1976.

———. *The Correspondence of the Van Cortlandt Family of Cortlandt Manor, 1748–1800.* Van Cortlandt Family Papers, Vol. 2. Tarrytown, New York, 1977.

Reynolds, Helen Wilkinson. *Dutch Houses in the Hudson Valley Before 1776.* New York, 1929.

Scharf, J. Thomas, ed. *History of Westchester County, New York.* 2 Vols. Philadelphia, 1886.

Schuyler, Montgomery. *The Patrons and Lords of Manors on the Hudson.* New York, 1932.

Singleton, Esther. *The Furniture of Our Forefathers.* New York, 1901.